SPOT 50
Wild
Animals

Sally Morgan

Miles KelL

First published in 2011 by Miles Kelly Publishing Ltd
Harding's Barn, Bardfield End Green, Thaxted, Essex, CM6 3PX, UK

2 4 6 8 10 9 7 5 3 1

Publishing Director Belinda Gallagher

Creative Director Jo Cowan

Editors Amanda Askew, Sarah Parkin

Designer Kayleigh Allen

Production Manager Elizabeth Collins

Reprographics Stephan Davis, Ian Paulyn

ISBN 978-1-84810-448-8

Printed in China

British Library Cataloguing-in-Publication Data
A catalogue record for this book is available from the British Library

ACKNOWLEDGEMENTS
The publishers would like to thank the artist Ian Jackson who has contributed to this book

All other images are from the Miles Kelly Archives

Made with paper from a sustainable forest

www.mileskelly.net
info@mileskelly.net

www.factsforprojects.com
The one-stop homework helper — pictures, facts, videos, projects and more

Self-publish your
children's book

buddingpress.co.uk

CONTENTS

Tick the circles when you have spotted the species.

HABITATS

Some animals live in the wild, without humans, and are not tame. They are found in many habitats around the world. The habitat is the type of environment in which they live, such as a forest or desert.

Grasslands are areas of flat land, such as the African savannah, where there is lots of grass and few trees.

Deserts are dry places that get little rain. Some deserts, such as the Sahara, are hot and covered in sand.

Forests and rainforests are places with lots of trees. They are home to many different animals.

Mountains are highlands where it can become so cold, snow covers the slopes for many months.

Polar regions at the North and South poles are extremely cold and covered in ice.

Oceans and fresh water cover much of the world and are home to fish and many other aquatic animals.

ANIMAL GROUPS

Animals can be divided into two main groups, invertebrates **and vertebrates.** Invertebrates such as insects do not have a backbone, but vertebrates such as mammals do. There are more than 50,000 species, or types, of vertebrate and they are among the most advanced and intelligent animals on the planet.

▶ *A skeleton supports and protects an animal's body.*

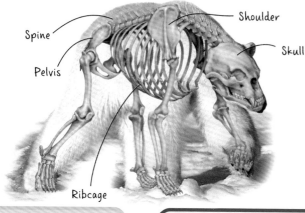

Shoulder

Spine

Skull

Pelvis

Ribcage

VERTEBRATES

In this book, you can learn about 50 vertebrates that live in the wild. Vertebrates are split into the following groups.

FISH

These animals live in water. Their body is covered in scales and they breathe using gills. They have fins, rather than limbs, which they use to swim through water.

MAMMALS

Intelligent animals, mammals are covered in hair. Most females give birth to live young, apart from a few that lay eggs. They feed their young with milk.

REPTILES

With scaly skin, most reptiles have four legs, but snakes and some lizards are legless. Some reptiles lay leathery eggs, but others give birth to live young.

BIRDS

Covered in feathers, most birds can fly using their wings. They have two legs that they use to perch and a beak (or bill) rather than teeth. Females lay shelled eggs.

AMPHIBIANS

Most amphibians have four legs. They live in and near water. Their skin is moist and lacks scales. They lay eggs, which hatch into tadpoles. The tadpoles change into adults.

ANTEATER

With no teeth, anteaters feed only on ants and termites. Their long tongue is covered in tiny, backward-pointing spines and sticky saliva for licking up prey. They have long, sharp claws to open ant and termite nests. However, their claws make it difficult to walk. They tuck them under their feet and walk on their knuckles, which makes it look as if they are limping. There are four species, including the giant anteater.

SCALE

The giant anteater's tongue is 60 cm long and it flicks out up to 150 times a minute to scoop up ants.

FACT FILE

Common name Giant anteater
Latin name
Myrmecophaga tridactyla
Size 2 m (body length, inc. tail)
Habitat Tropical grasslands and Central and South American forests
Life span About 14 years

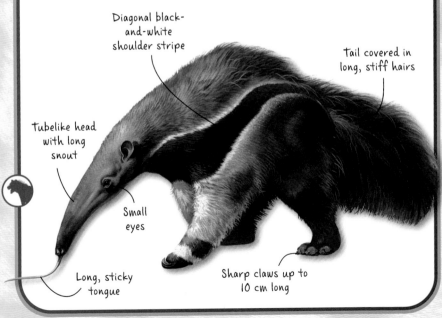

Diagonal black-and-white shoulder stripe

Tail covered in long, stiff hairs

Tubelike head with long snout

Small eyes

Long, sticky tongue

Sharp claws up to 10 cm long

BABOON

These monkeys live in large groups called troops, headed by a male. They spend much of the day on the ground in search of food, but climb trees to sleep or escape from predators. Baboons walk on all four legs. When they feed, they stand on one hand and pick up food with the other. They are noisy monkeys that communicate using barks, screeches and yelps. A particularly loud bark is used to warn others of danger. There are five species, including the yellow baboon.

SCALE

The canine teeth of the baboon can be longer than those of the lion.

FACT FILE

Common name Yellow baboon
Latin name *Papio cynocephalus*
Size 70 cm (body length)
Habitat Tropical grasslands and forests of east Africa
Life span 14 to 27 years

Grey-brown hair, longer over the shoulders

Dark, hairless, doglike face

Pointed nose

Hand with four fingers and a thumb

Long tail

BAT

The only animals that are able to fly are bats, birds and insects. Bats have wings rather than arms, and each wing is covered in skin and supported by extra long fingers. Bats are generally nocturnal and they navigate in the dark using echolocation. Most bats hunt insects, but a few catch fish and frogs, while others feed on fruit and nectar. There are more than 900 species in the world – that's one in every five mammal species.

SCALE

The vampire bat is a bloodsucker. It bites through skin using its sharp incisor teeth and then laps up the blood that oozes out.

FACT FILE

Common name
Brown long-eared bat
Latin name *Plecotus auritus*
Size 5 cm (body length);
25 cm (wingspan)
Habitat Woodlands, parks and gardens across Europe and Asia
Life span 5 to 22 years

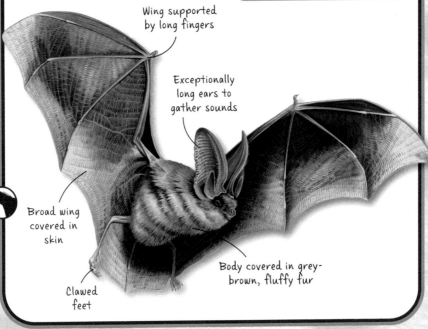

Wing supported by long fingers

Exceptionally long ears to gather sounds

Broad wing covered in skin

Body covered in grey-brown, fluffy fur

Clawed feet

BEAR

Carnivorous mammals, bears use curved claws for digging and ripping up wood. Bears walk on the soles of their feet, placing the whole foot on the ground when they walk, just like humans. Some of the smaller bears are good at climbing. Brown and black bears eat a mixed diet of fruit, nuts, grasses, insects and fish. Bears don't have great eyesight, but they have an excellent sense of smell. There are eight species, including the American black bear.

SCALE

Some bears associate people with food, so they hunt for food on rubbish dumps and raid campsites.

FACT FILE

Common name
American black bear

Latin name *Ursus americanus*

Size 2 m (body length)

Habitat Forests and mountains of North America

Life span Up to 30 years

Longer claws on front feet

Rounded ears with short fur

Small eyes

Long, pale muzzle

Body covered in shaggy, black fur

Broad, flat feet with five claws

CHEETAH

Reaching speeds of 115 km/h, cheetahs are **the fastest land animal.** This big cat is a predator of gazelle, impala, warthogs, rabbits and birds. Most females live on their own, except when they have babies. Young males live in small groups called coalitions. Cheetahs often sit in trees or on termite mounds to get a good look at the surrounding savannah. Once they have spotted prey, they creep up on them, until they are just 50 m away and then give chase.

The cheetah can run 32 m in just a second. It uses its tail to steer and balance its body.

FACT FILE

Common name Cheetah

Latin name *Acinonyx jubatus*

Size 130 cm (body length);
85 cm (height to shoulder)

Habitat Savannah of
sub-Saharan Africa

Life span Up to 14 years

Up to six black rings on the last third of the tail

Black teardrop under each eye

Small head with short ears

White throat

Tawny fur with black spots

Pale underside

Slender, streamlined body with long legs

CHIMPANZEE

Intelligent and social animals, chimps live in forests feeding on a varied diet of fruit, insects, birds and small mammals. They have a stout body with a sloping back and long arms that reach to their knees when they stand. Chimps walk over the ground on all fours, supporting themselves on their knuckles. They are also good at climbing trees. They live in groups that can number anything from 15 to more than 100 individuals.

SCALE

Chimps have learned to use tools such as sticks to get ants out of their nests.

FACT FILE

Common name Chimpanzee
Latin name *Pan troglodytes*
Size 85 cm (body length)
Habitat Tropical rainforests of central and west Africa
Life span 40 to 45 years

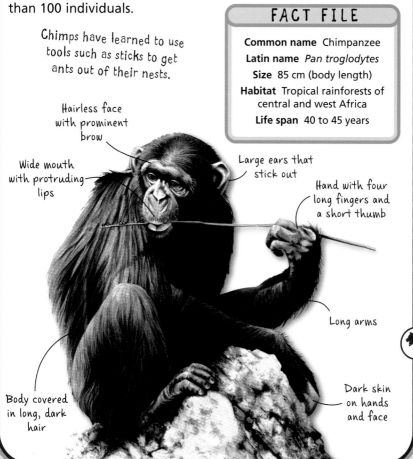

Hairless face with prominent brow

Wide mouth with protruding lips

Large ears that stick out

Hand with four long fingers and a short thumb

Long arms

Body covered in long, dark hair

Dark skin on hands and face

DEER

Hoofed mammals, deer have long legs that are adapted to running. They are herbivores that feed on grass, leaves and other plants. They also eat nuts and berries. Deer are social animals that usually live in herds. Males have antlers made of bone, which range in shape from simple spikes to elaborate branches. They regrow a new set of antlers each year. There are about 44 species, including the fallow deer.

SCALE

The smallest deer species is the Andean pudi, which weighs just 10 kg. The largest is the moose that weighs about 800 kg.

FACT FILE

Common name Fallow deer

Latin name *Dama dama*

Size 85 cm (height to shoulder)

Habitat Woodlands of Europe and the Middle East; introduced to Australia and Americas

Life span 12 to 16 years

Large, branched, palm-shaped antlers

Fawn-coloured coat with white spots

Black line down the tail

White patch edged with black under the tail

White underside

Legs end in hooves

DOLPHIN

SCALE

Unlike fish, which have gills to breathe in water, dolphins are marine mammals with lungs, so they have to come to the surface to breathe. They are social animals that live in groups of up to 1000 individuals. They are expert swimmers, moving quickly through the water after fish and squid. They can somersault and spin above the water, too. They are very intelligent and communicate with each other using clicks and whistles. There are 32 species, including the common dolphin.

Dolphins do not close both eyes when they sleep. They close one eye for about 10 minutes and then the other.

FACT FILE

Common name
Common dolphin
Latin name *Delphinus delphis*
Size 2.5 m (body length)
Habitat Tropical, warm coastal and open waters
Life span 35 to 40 years

Flukes pointed at tips, with central notch

Triangular dorsal fin

Dark circles around the eyes, with a dark line running between them

Dark-grey to black upper body

Light-grey to yellow sides

Long flippers

Black line from jaws to flipper

Elongated beak

ELEPHANT

The largest, living land animals are elephants. They live in herds of related females and their young. Each herd is led by the oldest female, called the matriarch. A female is pregnant for 22 months and gives birth to a single calf. Males live alone or in small bachelor groups. Elephants are plant eaters, feeding on leaves, grass, roots and fruit. There are three species – the African Savannah, African forest and Asian.

SCALE

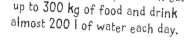

An adult African elephant can eat up to 300 kg of food and drink almost 200 l of water each day.

FACT FILE

Common name
African Savannah elephant

Latin name *Loxodonta africana*

Size 3 m (height to shoulder)

Habitat Savannah and forests of sub-Saharan Africa

Life span Up to 70 years

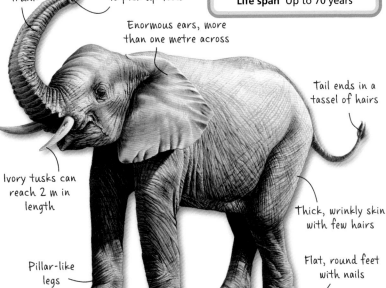

Long, flexible trunk

Finger-like tip to pick up food

Enormous ears, more than one metre across

Tail ends in a tassel of hairs

Ivory tusks can reach 2 m in length

Thick, wrinkly skin with few hairs

Pillar-like legs

Flat, round feet with nails

GIBBON

Using their long arms, gibbons swing through the trees at a speed of 3 m/sec. This is called brachiation. They are very active animals, and can walk along branches and leap across gaps between trees. When they are on the ground, they walk on two feet. Gibbons are forest primates and live in small family groups of between two and six individuals. They are active during the day and feed on leaves, shoots and fruit such as figs. There are 11 species of gibbon.

SCALE

Gibbons are very noisy. The sound of the lar gibbon, a mix of whoops and hoots, can carry more than one kilometre through the rainforest.

FACT FILE

Common name Lar gibbon
Latin name *Hylobates lar*
Size 90 cm (height)
Habitat Tropical forests of Southeast Asia
Life span 25 to 30 years

Long, thin arms and legs

White ring around black face

Light-brown, shaggy coat

Grasping fingers for hooking around branches

White hands and feet

No tail

GIRAFFE

Towering a massive 5.7 m above the ground, giraffes are the tallest land animal. They are so tall that their heads stick up above the trees on which they feed. Their spotted coat provides good camouflage. Giraffes are social animals that live in groups of 10 to 20 individuals. They are active at dawn and dusk, and usually sleep during the night. They can sleep standing up with their head resting on their back leg. When escaping predators, they can run at speeds of up to 60 km/h.

SCALE

The giraffe has a black tongue, about 45 cm long, which it uses to reach the leaves at the top of trees.

FACT FILE

Common name
Reticulated giraffe

Latin name
Giraffa camelopardalis

Size 5.7 m (height to horn tips)

Habitat Savannah and woodland of east and south Africa

Life span Up to 25 years

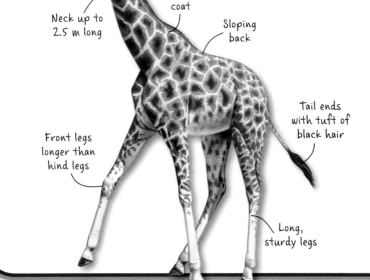

Pair of horns

Large eyes

Neck up to 2.5 m long

Spotted coat

Sloping back

Front legs longer than hind legs

Tail ends with tuft of black hair

Long, sturdy legs

GORILLA

One of our closest relatives, gorillas are the largest primates. They are intelligent animals that live in groups made up of related females and their young, and an adult male. Gorillas walk on all fours, using the soles of their hind feet and the knuckles of their hands. Young gorillas are good climbers. During the day, the group moves through the forest, feeding on leaves and then rests before moving on. At night they make a nest from leaves and branches. There are two species, the eastern and western.

SCALE

Mountain gorillas, a type of eastern gorilla, have a thick coat to keep them warm when temperatures fall at night.

FACT FILE

Common name Eastern gorilla
Latin name *Gorilla beringei*
Size 1.8 m (height)
Habitat Rainforests of central Africa
Life span 30 to 40 years

Massive head

Thick, dark fur over body

Stout body

Dark skin on face

Long, muscular arms

Broad hand with four fingers and a thumb

Short legs

HIPPOPOTAMUS

The fourth largest mammals are hippos. They spend the day floating in water with just their eyes and nostrils above the surface. Sometimes they sink and walk on the river bed. At night, they clamber from the water to graze on grass. Males usually live alone, but females and their young stay in herds of up to 30 animals. Males are dangerous animals, fighting over females and inflicting serious injuries on each other with their teeth.

SCALE

FACT FILE

Common name Hippopotamus
Latin name
Hippopotamus amphibius
Size 1.5 m (height);
5 m (body length)
Habitat Rivers and swamps in west and east Africa
Life span Up to 40 years

Hippos can outrun a human, reaching a top speed of 30 km/h.

Dark-brown, hairless skin

Round, barrel-like body

Ears and eyes on the top of the head

Short legs

Upward-pointing nostrils

18

HORSE

Wild horses are found in many parts of the world, for example, the Mustang of North America and the Brumby of Australia. Most wild horses are descendents of horses that escaped from people, but the Przewalski's horse has never been tamed and is a true wild horse. Horses live in herds of females, led by a stallion (male). Horses are grazing animals. Each day the herd travels several kilometres, feeding on fresh grass.

SCALE

Przewalski's horse is critically endangered with fewer than 100 living in the wild, although there are several thousand living in zoos.

FACT FILE

Common name
Takhi or Przewalski's horse

Latin name *Equus ferus przewalskii*

Size 1.3 m (height to shoulder); 2 m (body length)

Habitat Steppes of central Asia

Life span About 20 years

Stiff, dark-brown mane down the neck

Brown coat

Long face with powerful jaw

Tail about 90 cm long

Pale underside

HYENA

Working alone or in small groups, hyenas are skilled hunters. They prey on animals such as zebras, gazelle and hares. They are also scavengers, eating food left untouched by other animals. Their jaws can crack through the largest bones, so nothing is wasted. They fear few animals other than the lion. They live in family groups called clans. Each clan has a territory, which they defend against intruding clans. Females give birth to their cubs in an underground den.

SCALE

A spotted hyena can gorge itself with up to 15 kg of food, which it swallows quickly.

FACT FILE

Common name Spotted hyena

Latin name *Crocuta crocuta*

Size 1.3 m (body length inc. tail); 80 cm (height to shoulder)

Habitat Savannah, open woodland and desert in sub-Saharan Africa

Life span Up to 25 years

Thick neck and large head

Rounded ears

Mane of longer hairs down back

Sloping back

Coarse, shaggy coat

Powerful jaws

Yellow-grey coat with dark spots

Front legs longer than hind legs

Feet with four toes and claws

KANGAROO

Kangaroos are marsupials – mammals that have a pouch in which they raise their young. Their young are born after 33 days and are 2.5 cm long. The tiny baby crawls into its mother's pouch, where it attaches to a teat to suckle. Kangaroos have long hind legs to propel forwards at a speed of up to 60 km/h. They can also leap more than 8 m. Kangaroos are plant eaters, feeding on grass and other plants. There are four species of larger kangaroo and a number of smaller relatives.

SCALE

A group of kangaroos is called a mob. Some mobs number as many as 1500 individuals.

FACT FILE

Common name Red kangaroo

Latin name *Macropus rufus*

Size 1.5 m (body length); 1.2 m (tail length)

Habitat Open woodland, grassland and desert of central Australia

Life span 7 to 15 years

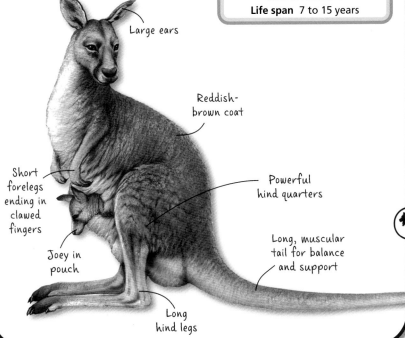

Large ears

Reddish-brown coat

Short forelegs ending in clawed fingers

Powerful hind quarters

Joey in pouch

Long, muscular tail for balance and support

Long hind legs

LEMUR

Found only on Madagascar and neighbouring islands, lemurs are small primates. There are more than ten different lemur species. Most are cat-sized animals with a long tail. Their hind limbs are longer than their forelimbs, which helps them to climb trees. They move through forests with ease, running along branches and leaping from tree to tree. Some lemurs are fruit eaters, others eat leaves or insects, and one species eats only the leaves of the bamboo plant.

SCALE

The aye-aye, a type of lemur, pulls fat grubs from rotting logs using its extra long claw.

FACT FILE

Common name
Ringtailed lemur

Latin name *Lemur catta*

Size 40 cm (body length);
60 cm (tail length)

Habitat Forests of Madagascar

Life span Up to 18 years

Long, banded tail

Reddish-brown back

White face with triangular black markings

Amber eyes

Black nose

Grey-brown legs

White underside

LEOPARD

Solitary creatures, leopards prey on small animals such as deer, antelope, rabbits and birds. They hunt from dusk to dawn. Sometimes they creep up on their prey, other times they ambush them. During the day, they rest in trees where they are safe and shaded from the sun. Their spots provide excellent camouflage, especially when in trees. There is only one species of leopard, but several sub-species, such as the Amur and North African leopard.

SCALE

FACT FILE

Common name Leopard
Latin name *Panthera pardus*
Size 1.5 m (body length);
75 cm (height to shoulder)
Habitat Forests, mountains, grassland and desert of south Asia and sub-Saharan Africa
Life span Up to 10 years

Leopards drag their kill into trees where they are out of reach of other predators and scavengers.

Short ears

Black spots on orange-brown fur

Long whiskers

Long, muscular body

Pale underside with spots

Black blotches on the belly

Tail about 80 cm long

LION

Due to their size and power, lions are often called the 'king of beasts'. They are strong enough to catch and kill large prey such as zebras and wildebeest, as well as gazelle, antelope and birds. They live in groups called prides, made up of a male and several lionesses with young. Lionesses give birth to up to six cubs every two years. The cubs stay with the pride until they are about 16 months old, when the males leave. There is a sub-species called the Asiatic lion that lives in the Gir forest of India.

The lion's tongue is rough like sandpaper. This helps to grip prey and to pull bits of meat off bones.

FACT FILE

Common name African lion

Latin name *Panthera leo*

Size 2.7 m (body length); 1.2 m (height to shouder)

Habitat Savannah and semi-deserts of sub-Saharan Africa

Life span Up to 10 years

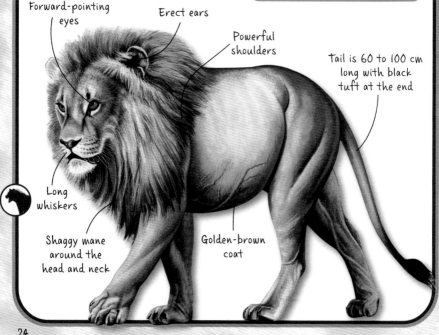

Forward-pointing eyes

Erect ears

Powerful shoulders

Tail is 60 to 100 cm long with black tuft at the end

Long whiskers

Shaggy mane around the head and neck

Golden-brown coat

MEERKAT

Small mammals, meerkats live together in family groups called packs. Each pack consists of several breeding pairs and their offspring. Meerkats live in underground burrows. During the day, they emerge from their burrows to hunt for food such as insects, spiders, small lizards and eggs. There is always a meerkat on guard duty, watching for predators such as eagles, jackals and snakes. There is great rivalry between neighbouring packs and they often fight.

SCALE

In the morning, meerkats stand up and face the sun so that the black patch on their belly can absorb heat.

FACT FILE

Common name Meerkat
Latin name *Suricata suricatta*
Size 25 cm (body length)
Habitat Deserts of southern Africa
Life span 5 to 15 years

Narrow, tapered face with pointed nose

Fingers with claws

Feet with four toes each

Long, thin tail with black tip

Yellow-brown coat

25

ORANG-UTAN

Solitary primates, orang-utans are one of the largest animals that can climb trees. They are active during the day, swinging from branch to branch, only coming to the ground to cross open ground. At night, they build a platform of branches to sleep on. Orang-utans feed mostly on fruit, but also eat leaves, bark and flowers. They collect water from holes in trees. There are two species, the Bornean and the Sumatran.

SCALE

Orang-utans have very long arms – the length of each arm is the same as the height of a five-year-old child.

FACT FILE

Common name
Bornean orang-utan

Latin name *Pongo pygmaeus*

Size 1.5 m (height)

Habitat Tropical rainforests of Southeast Asia

Life span 50 to 60 years

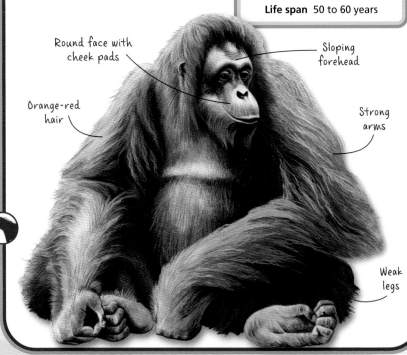

Round face with cheek pads

Sloping forehead

Orange-red hair

Strong arms

Weak legs

PANDA

SCALE

These forest-living mammals spend up to **12 hours a day eating bamboo**. They have to eat as much as 20 kg a day because bamboo is a poor-quality plant food. They have large, ridged teeth to grind up the tough bamboo and an extra wrist bone that's like a small thumb, which helps them to handle the bamboo shoots. Females give birth to one or two cubs in August to September. The cubs stay with their mother until they are about 18 months old.

The black–and–white markings provide camouflage in the snow, and help to break up the bear's outline so they are more difficult to spot.

FACT FILE

Common name Giant panda

Latin name
Ailuropoda melanoleuca

Size 1.7 m (body length); 70 cm (height to shoulder)

Habitat Forests in China

Life span Up to 25 years

Black ears

Round, white face with black rings around the eyes

Powerful jaws

Black limbs and white body

Stocky body

27

POLAR BEAR

Recognized by their white fur, polar bears are the largest, living land carnivores. They roam the icy Arctic and are expert predators, hunting seals, small whales and fish such as salmon. They are solitary animals, except for females with cubs. Females give birth to cubs in a den under the snow in the middle of winter and stay in the den until spring. Cubs remain with their mother for up to 3 years.

SCALE

A polar bear's insulation is so good that they can overheat on warm days, so they lie on the snow to get cool.

FACT FILE

Common name Polar bear

Latin name *Ursus maritimus*

Size 2.5 m (body length); 1.6 m (height to shoulder)

Habitat Tundra and ice floes of the Arctic

Life span 15 to 18 years

Small, rounded ears

Black nose

Stocky body

Thick, shaggy, white fur

Large front feet with claws

Hairy soles of feet

RHINOCEROS

These large mammals have either one or two horns. The horn is made from keratin, which also forms fingernails. Rhinos have poor sight and rely on their senses of smell and hearing. There are five types of rhino, including the black rhino. They are all plant eaters – feeding on grass and leaves. Most are solitary animals, but white rhinos pair up and may be seen in small groups.

SCALE

The white rhino is not white in colour. The name comes from the African word 'widje', which refers to their wide mouth.

FACT FILE

Common name Black rhino

Latin name *Diceros bicornis*

Size 3.5 m (body length); 1.6 m (height to shoulder)

Habitat Desert, savannah and forest across southern Africa

Life span 30 to 40 years

Thick, hairless skin

Tubelike ears

Two horns, one larger than the other

Small eyes either side of the head

Pointed upper lip

Short, sturdy legs

Three toes on each foot

SEAL

Adapted to a watery life, seals have flippers instead of legs, and a sleek streamlined body. They are marine mammals that live in water, but come onto land to give birth. Seals are clumsy on land, pulling themselves along with their flippers, but in the water they are agile swimmers. They can stay underwater for an hour or more, before returning to the surface to breathe. They hunt fish, shellfish and squid. There are 19 different species of seal.

SCALE

FACT FILE

Common name Harp seal
Latin name
Pagophilus groenlandicus
Size 1.8 m (body length)
Habitat Arctic and North Atlantic Ocean
Life span 30 to 35 years

The largest seal is the elephant seal, named after its huge proboscis (nose), which it uses to make roaring sounds.

Black head

Thick fur

Round eyes

Harp-shaped markings on the back

Hind flipper

Long whiskers

White fur of seal pup

SLOTH

Slow-moving sloths are solitary animals that live in trees. They hang underneath branches, gripping with their long, hooked claws. Sloths do not have good eyesight or hearing, so rely on their sense of smell to find plant food. They are rarely seen on the ground as their claws prevent them from walking, so they have to drag themselves along. However, they are good swimmers. There are six species, found in Central and South America.

SCALE

The long coat of the sloth is often covered in mites, ticks and beetles, as well as algae.

FACT FILE

Common name
Brown throated three-toed sloth

Latin name *Bradypus variegatus*

Size 50 cm (body length)

Habitat Tropical rainforests of South America

Life span Up to 30 years

Forelimbs longer than hind limbs

Three curved claws on each foot

Black hairs around eyes give a mask appearance

Small head

Dense, shaggy coat

TIGER

Preying on deer, wild pigs and buffalo, tigers are solitary predators that hunt mainly at night. They creep up on their prey and leap forwards, pushing the animal to the ground. Females give birth to two or three cubs that stay with her until they are 1.5 to 3 years old, during which time they learn to hunt. There is only one species of tiger but eight sub-species including the Bengal and Siberian. The largest is the Siberian tiger.

SCALE

A tiger's stripes are like fingerprints as no other tiger has the exact same pattern.

FACT FILE

Common name Siberian tiger
Latin name
Panthera tigris altaica
Size 3 m (body length);
110 cm (height to shoulder)
Habitat Forests of eastern Siberia
Life span 8 to 10 years

Tail with black rings

Red-orange coat with vertical black stripes

Extra long hairs around head

Forward-pointing eyes

Long whiskers

Pale, almost white, underside

Powerful shoulders and thick neck

WHALE

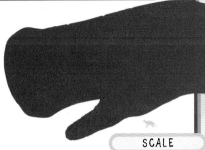

Giants of the oceans, whales are mammals, not fish, yet they live their entire life in water. They have lungs, so they have to come to the surface to breathe. They have a streamlined shape, virtually no hair and flippers rather than legs. There are two main types of whale. Baleen whales filter plankton and krill from the water, and toothed whales hunt animals such as fish, squid and seals.

SCALE

The blue whale is the world's largest animal. It grows to about 29 m and eats 4 tonnes of food each day.

FACT FILE

Common name Sperm whale

Latin name *Physeter macrocephalus*

Size 19 m (body length)

Habitat Temperate oceans, to depths of 3000 m

Life span Up to 70 years

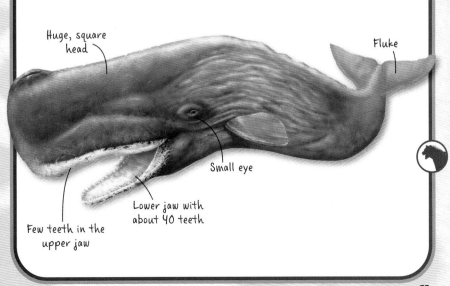

Huge, square head

Fluke

Small eye

Lower jaw with about 40 teeth

Few teeth in the upper jaw

WOLF

Found mostly in forests of the Northern Hemisphere, wolves are fearsome predators. They live in packs of up to nine individuals, sometimes more, which are lead by a top dog and top bitch. Only the top bitch has cubs and the other females in the pack help her to rear them. Wolves hunt together, catching caribou and other deer, rabbits and birds. Each pack occupies a territory that they patrol and defend against other wolves.

SCALE

Wolves howl to tell each other where they are, as well as before and after hunting. Sometimes they howl together.

FACT FILE

Common name Grey wolf

Latin name *Canis lupus*

Size 1.3 m (body length); 75 cm (height to shoulder)

Habitat Forests and mountains of North America, Europe, the Middle East and Asia

Life span 6 to 13 years

Erect ears

Forward-pointing eyes

Cheek hairs form tufts

Longer hairs around the neck and along the back

Coat colour is a mixture of white, grey, brown and black

Thick fur

Front foot with five toes

Hind foot with four toes

ZEBRA

Distinctive black-and-white stripes make zebras easy to identify. They are grazing mammals, feeding on grass. Zebras live in family groups made up of one stallion, about six females and their young. Zebras often walk in single file, with the top female at the front, followed by the other females in age order, and the male at the back to guard the group. At night one member of the group remains awake to watch for predators. There are three species.

SCALE

FACT FILE

Common name Plains zebra

Latin name *Equus quagga*

Size 2.3 m (body length); 120 cm (height to shoulder)

Habitat Open savannah of southeast Africa

Life span 12 years

Newborn foals have shaggy fur with pale-brown stripes, which make it difficult for predators to spot them.

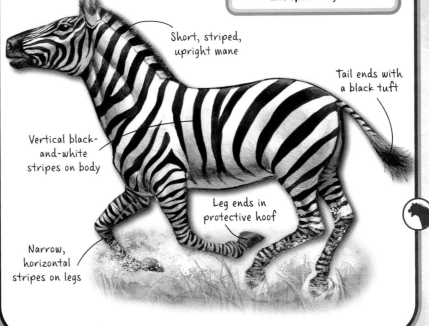

Short, striped, upright mane

Tail ends with a black tuft

Vertical black-and-white stripes on body

Leg ends in protective hoof

Narrow, horizontal stripes on legs

EAGLE

Among the largest and most powerful of
birds, eagles are found on every continent
except Antarctica. They are birds of prey that
hunt a variety of animals including mammals,
birds, reptiles, fish, bats and invertebrates.
Many eagles pair for life, returning to the
same nest site every year. Some nest high
above the ground on cliffs and in trees, but a
few nest on the ground. Males and females
look the same, but youngsters have
a different plumage.

SCALE

FACT FILE

Common name Golden eagle

Latin name *Aquila chrysaetos*

Size 85 cm (body length);
2 m (wingspan)

Habitat Grasslands, forests and
tundra across the Northern
Hemisphere

Life span About 30 years

An eagle's wing feathers are
separated at the tips to help
the air pass over the wing
and make flight smoother.

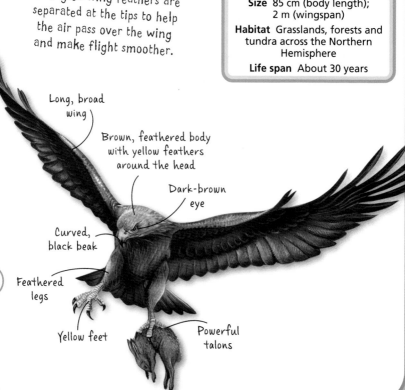

Long, broad
wing

Brown, feathered body
with yellow feathers
around the head

Dark-brown
eye

Curved,
black beak

Feathered
legs

Yellow feet

Powerful
talons

HUMMINGBIRD

By rapidly flapping their wings, hummingbirds are able to hover. This allows them to insert their long beaks into flowers to feed on sugary nectar. Hovering uses a lot of energy, so they have to eat their own weight in nectar every day. They also feed on insects and spiders. There are more than 300 species of these small, brightly coloured birds. The smallest weighs just 2 g.

SCALE

These birds get their name from the way their wings beat so fast – as many as 100 times a second, creating a humming sound.

FACT FILE

Common name
Crimson topaz hummingbird

Latin name *Topaza pella*

Size 20 cm (body length)

Habitat Tropical rainforests of South America

Life span 3 to 4 years

Fast-beating wings

Curved beak

Throat patch

Iridescent red underside

Tail feathers cross halfway down

OWL

Predatory birds with silent flight, owls hunt animals such as small mammals, lizards, birds and fish. Most owls are nocturnal, hunting at night and roosting during the day. They have excellent hearing and vision, even in low light. Most owls live and hunt alone. They do not build their own nests, but use holes in trees and walls. There are more than 200 species, which are found around the world in virtually all habitats.

SCALE

Owls can hear the rustling sounds of small animals moving through leaves on the forest floor.

FACT FILE

Common name Barn owl
Latin name *Tyto alba*
Size 40 cm (body length)
Habitat Grassland and farmland, on all continents except Antarctica
Life span 1 to 5 years

Brown head and back

Heart-shaped face

Flight feathers on long wing

Large, forward-facing eyes

Hooked beak

Talon

Feathered legs to the toes

Grey-white underside

PENGUIN

Although penguins have wings, they are unable to fly. Their wings are modified to form flippers for swimming. They are expert swimmers that spend much of their life at sea where they hunt small fish, squid and krill. These social birds return to land to breed, often forming large colonies. They are found in the Southern Hemisphere from the Galapagos to the Antarctic. There are 17 species. The largest is the Emperor penguin, which is more than one metre tall and weighs up to 35 kg.

SCALE

The Emperor penguin can stay underwater for up to 18 minutes and dive to depths of 500 m.

FACT FILE

Common name
Humboldt penguin
Latin name
Spheniscus humboldti
Size 75 cm (height)
Habitat Rocky coasts of Chile and Peru
Life span 15 to 20 years

Pink mark behind beak

White band around head

Black upside-down horseshoe shape on chest

Stiff flipper-like wings

Claws

Webbed feet

TOUCAN

Most toucans use their extra-large beak to pick fruit from branches to eat. They also feed on insects, young birds and lizards. They are usually seen in pairs or in small groups. Toucans nest in small holes in trees, often using the same hole for many years. The hole is small so the adults have to fold their tail feathers over their back to fit. There are about 40 species of toucan.

SCALE

The huge beak of the toucan looks heavy but it is honeycombed with air spaces so it is very light.

FACT FILE

Common name Toco toucan

Latin name *Ramphastos toco*

Size 65 cm (body length inc. beak); 20 cm (beak)

Habitat Tropical forests and grasslands of eastern South America

Life span Up to 20 years

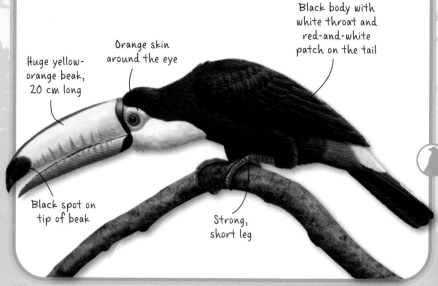

Black body with white throat and red-and-white patch on the tail

Orange skin around the eye

Huge yellow-orange beak, 20 cm long

Black spot on tip of beak

Strong, short leg

ALLIGATOR

Large reptiles, alligators prey on animals such as fish, mammals and turtles. They have few natural enemies apart from some of the larger snakes. Females build a mound in which they lay their leathery eggs. The eggs hatch after a couple of months. The young stay with the female for up to 2 years. There are eight species of alligator and their close relatives the caimans.

SCALE

Alligators have between 74 and 80 teeth, which are replaced all the time. They can go through as many as 3000 teeth in a lifetime.

FACT FILE

Common name
American alligator

Latin name
Alligator mississippiensis

Size 4 m (body length)

Habitat Swamps of southeast USA

Life span 35 to 50 years

Long,
powerful tail

Scutes (bony plates)
down the back

Four toes on
hind feet

Scaly skin

Lower teeth hidden
when mouth closed

Broad,
blunt snout

COBRA

Aggressive in nature, cobras are venomous snakes. They rear up when threatened and flatten the ribs in their neck to form their characteristic hood. They can strike any animal or person within a couple of metres. They detect moving prey, such as small mammals, birds and lizards, using their eyesight as well as vibrations in the ground. When they bite, their venom passes through channels in their fangs into the bite. The animal dies quickly and is swallowed whole.

SCALE

Cobras are common in areas where there are lots of people so thousands die from their bites each year.

FACT FILE

Common name King cobra

Latin name
Ophiophagus hannah

Size 4 m (body length)

Habitat Forests across south and Southeast Asia

Life span 20 years

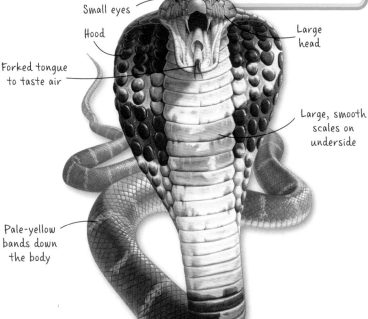

Small eyes

Hood

Forked tongue
to taste air

Large
head

Large, smooth
scales on
underside

Pale-yellow
bands down
the body

CROCODILE

These large reptiles have long jaws that can open wide and catch prey such as fish, deer, antelope and birds. They have an armoured appearance and spend most of the time in water looking for prey, with just their eyes and nostrils above the surface. They tend to crawl over land, although they can raise their body off the ground and gallop for short distances. There are 14 species of crocodile. They lay their eggs in mounds of vegetation near water.

SCALE

When Nile crocodiles open their mouth to keep cool, birds called Egyptian plovers hop in to clean their teeth.

FACT FILE

Common name Nile crocodile
Latin name
Crocodylus niloticus
Size 5 m (body length)
Habitat Rivers and swamps
Life span 45 years or more

Long, powerful tail

Green eyes

Scutes (bony plates) down back

Eye on top of the head

Long snout

Fourth tooth on lower jaw sticks out

FROG

Tail-less amphibians, frogs have long hind legs for jumping. Their thin, moist skin restricts them to damp habitats near water. They feed on small animals such as insects, slugs and worms, which they catch with their long, sticky tongue. Poison dart frogs are incredibly poisonous – their bright colours being a warning of their toxicity. Most frogs lay their eggs in water. The eggs hatch into tadpoles, which undergo a change in appearance to become adults. This is called metamorphosis.

SCALE

The most poisonous frog is the golden poison dart frog. It contains enough poison to kill ten adult men.

FACT FILE

Common name
Strawberry poison dart frog

Latin name *Oophaga pummilio*

Size 2 cm (body length)

Habitat Rainforests in Central America

Life span Up to 15 years

Bulging eyes

Red body

Short back

Long hind legs

Wide mouth

Shorter forelegs with four toes

Blue legs

IGUANA

Found in trees or among rocks, iguanas are large lizards. They vary in colour from brown to green. Iguanas have a third 'eye' – a patch on the top of their head that is sensitive to light. Males have a dewlap – a skin flap under their throat that they can inflate to signal to others. Females lay up to 70 eggs in their nest. The hatchlings live in trees when they are young. There are about 35 species.

SCALE

The skin of the banded iguana can change colour to match its surroundings.

FACT FILE

Common name Banded iguana

Latin name
Brachylophus fasciatus

Size 60 cm (body length)

Habitat Island habitats across the Pacific Ocean

Life span 15 years or more

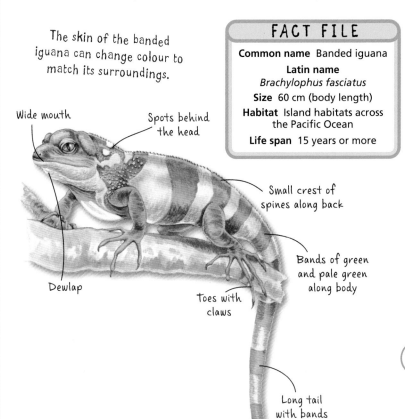

Wide mouth

Spots behind the head

Small crest of spines along back

Bands of green and pale green along body

Dewlap

Toes with claws

Long tail with bands

KOMODO DRAGON

The world's largest lizards are **komodo dragons.** Despite their size, they are agile and can move quickly, and even swim. Komodo dragons hunt deer, goats and pigs. They have an incredible sense of smell and can find rotting bodies from several kilometres away. Females lay their eggs in a nest. The hatchlings live in trees for several years to escape the adults that prey on them. They move to the ground when they are large enough to defend themselves.

SCALE

The komodo's saliva contains so many harmful bacteria that any animals wounded by the lizard usually get an infection and die.

FACT FILE

Common name Komodo dragon
Latin name
Varanus komodoensis
Size 3 m (body length)
Habitat Dry grasslands of Indonesia
Life span 20 to 40 years

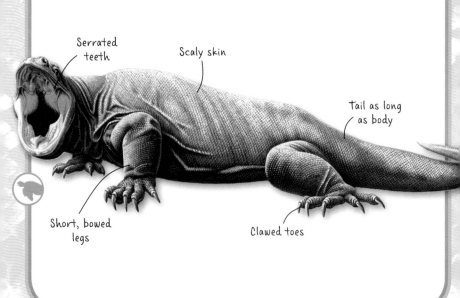

Serrated teeth

Scaly skin

Tail as long as body

Short, bowed legs

Clawed toes

PYTHON

Called constricting snakes, pythons kill their prey by wrapping themselves around their victim's body and suffocating it. Like all snakes, pythons can open their mouth very wide because their lower jaw can dislocate. They do not chew, but swallow their prey whole. Females lay a clutch of leathery eggs, which hatch after about two months. Some pythons care for their eggs by wrapping their body around them for warmth. There are about 27 species of python.

SCALE

FACT FILE

Common name
Reticulated python

Latin name *Python reticulatus*

Size 4 m (body length)

Habitat Tropical forests

Life span 10 years

The reticulated python is the longest snake. Most are 3 to 4 m long, but some are known to have reached 10 m.

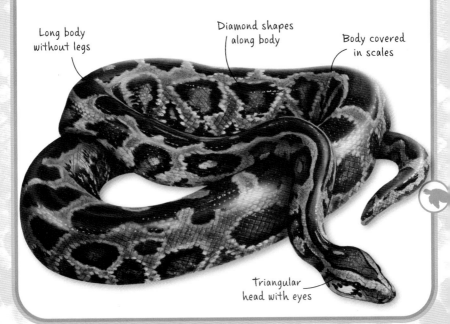

Long body without legs

Diamond shapes along body

Body covered in scales

Triangular head with eyes

SALAMANDER

Salamanders are amphibians with tails. They need to keep their skin moist so they live in damp places near water. There are more than 55 species of salamander. Some live in water all the time, while others just return to water to breed. They lay eggs that hatch into tadpoles. Adults hunt prey such as insects, spiders and worms, while tadpoles eat small animals in the water.

SCALE

FACT FILE

Common name Fire salamander

Latin name
Salamandra salamandra

Size 20 cm (body length)

Habitat Forests of central and southern Europe

Life span Up to 20 years

Salamanders can regrow their tail if it is damaged.

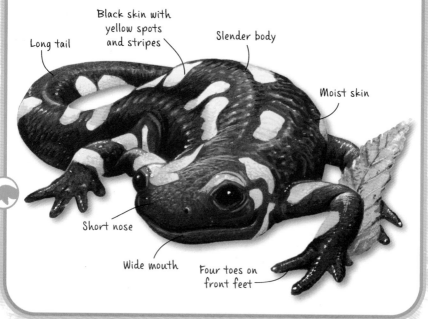

Long tail

Black skin with yellow spots and stripes

Slender body

Moist skin

Short nose

Wide mouth

Four toes on front feet

TOAD

With a more rounded body than frogs, toads tend to crawl rather than jump. They are amphibians with short, stocky legs and no tail. Their skin is usually dry with warts. Just behind the eyes, there is a distinctive parotoid gland that secretes a foul-tasting, poisonous liquid to deter predators. Toads lay their eggs in water and they hatch into tadpoles. There are about 150 species of toad.

SCALE

FACT FILE

Common name
Natterjack toad

Latin name *Epidalea calamitia*

Size 7 cm (body length)

Habitat Heathlands of Northern Europe

Life span Up to 15 years

Many toads inflate their body when threatened to make themselves look larger.

Bulging eyes

Horizontal, black pupil in eye

Dry skin with warts

Wide mouth

Short legs

Four toes on front feet

Partially webbed hind feet

TURTLE

Adistinct protective shell covers the **body of turtles.** They are marine reptiles with powerful flippers for swimming. On land they are unable to lift their body, so have to crawl. Turtles feed on a variety of animals such as crabs, sea anemones, jellyfish, corals, algae and sponges. Females return to the beach where they were born to lay their eggs in the sand. The hatchlings appear after 40 to 70 days and make a dash to the sea.

SCALE

Green turtles get their name from the appearance of their flesh, not their shell.

FACT FILE

Common name Green turtle
Latin name *Chelonia mydas*
Size 1.5 m (body length)
Habitat Tropical oceans
Life span 80 years or more

Small head

Upper shell called carapace

Toothless beak

Tail

Lower shell called plastron

Paddle-like flippers

Greenish shell

PIRANHA

Freshwater fish of South America, piranhas have a row of razor-sharp teeth on both jaws. The top teeth interlock with bottom teeth so when they bite, they can rip off a mouthful of flesh at the same time. Piranhas prey on fish, insects and snails, as well as rotting carcasses. Small groups lurk in the shadows waiting to ambush prey that swim too close. There are about 40 different species of piranha.

SCALE

Shoals of piranha may attack large animals, but only if they are attracted by blood in the water.

FACT FILE

Common name
Red-bellied piranha

Latin name
Pygocentrus nattereri

Size 25 cm (body length)

Habitat Freshwater rivers of South America

Life span Up to 10 years

Red eye

Pointed, triangular teeth, close together

Silver-blue on top

Red-orange underside

RAY

Wide, flat-bodied fish, rays have large pectoral fins that stick out like wings from either side of their body. Like the shark, their skeleton is made of cartilage. Most rays live near or on the seabed and swim slowly, moving their pectoral fins up and down. Some partially bury themselves in the seabed where they lie in wait to ambush their prey, including fish and invertebrates such as molluscs and crabs. Others such as manta and eagle rays swim across oceans, feeding on plankton.

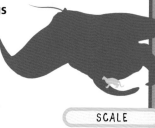

SCALE

Manta rays have large flaps either side of their head to funnel plankton into their mouth.

FACT FILE

Common name Manta ray
Latin name *Manta birostris*
Size 7 m (body length)
Habitat Tropical oceans to depths of 120 m
Life span 10 to 20 years

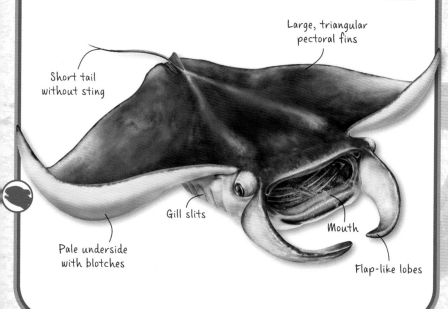

Large, triangular pectoral fins

Short tail without sting

Gill slits

Mouth

Pale underside with blotches

Flap-like lobes

SEAHORSE

Propelled by their dorsal fin, seahorses swim upright in the water. They are unusual fish that lack scales. Instead they have thin skin, stretched over bony plates to give them an armoured appearance. Their body shape provides good camouflage among seaweed, where they lie in wait for tiny prey such as brine shrimp, to pass by. When an animal is close enough, they suck it into their mouth. There are fewer than 40 species.

SCALE

The female lays her eggs inside the male's pouch. He carries the eggs until they hatch into miniature seahorses, which he releases into the water.

FACT FILE

Common name Spiny seahorse
Latin name
Hippocampus histrix
Size 15 cm (body length)
Habitat Shallow water in the western Pacific Ocean
Life span 1 to 5 years

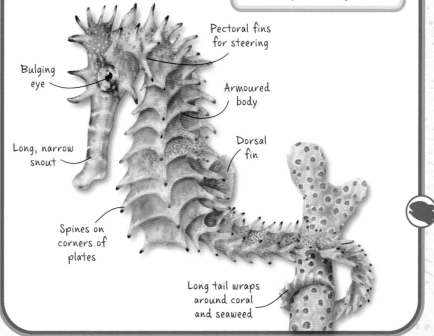

Pectoral fins for steering

Bulging eye

Armoured body

Long, narrow snout

Dorsal fin

Spines on corners of plates

Long tail wraps around coral and seaweed

SHARK

Despite being the most feared animals in the ocean, sharks are not all large and dangerous. Only ten species grow to more than 4 m long, but most are about one metre. Sharks are cartilaginous fish as they have a skeleton made of cartilage rather than bone. They are predators, feeding on animals such as fish, seals, dolphins, molluscs and birds. Some sharks are solitary, but others live in shoals.

SCALE

FACT FILE

Common name
Great white shark
Latin name
Carcharodon carcharias
Size 5 m (body length)
Habitat Coastal waters
of most oceans
Life span Up to 40 years

A few sharks lay large eggs, but most give birth to live young.

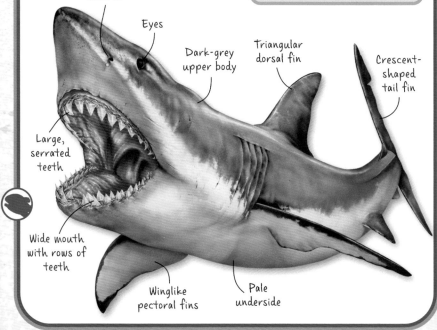

Nostrils

Eyes

Dark-grey
upper body

Triangular
dorsal fin

Crescent-
shaped
tail fin

Large,
serrated
teeth

Wide mouth
with rows of
teeth

Winglike
pectoral fins

Pale
underside

VIPERFISH

Bizarre-looking viperfish are one of the most ferocious animals of the deep ocean. They have a huge head armed with fangs that are so long, they do not fit in the mouth. These weapons allow them to prey on fish and crustaceans. The dorsal fin has a long, arching ray with a light-producing organ called a photophore at the end. Viperfish wiggle the lure to tempt prey animals to swim close to their mouth.

SCALE

The viperfish's stomach can expand to accommodate large prey animals.

FACT FILE

Common name Sloan's viperfish
Latin name *Chauliodus sloani*
Size 35 cm (body length)
Habitat Temperate and tropical oceans, to depths of 3000 m
Life span Unknown

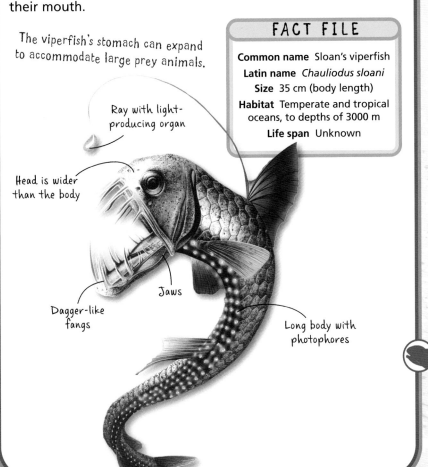

Ray with light-producing organ

Head is wider than the body

Jaws

Dagger-like fangs

Long body with photophores

GLOSSARY

Ambush When an animal lies in wait and suddenly attacks.

Aquatic Living in water.

Camouflaged When an animal is shaped, coloured or patterned to blend in with its surroundings.

Carcass The dead body of an animal.

Carnivore An animal that eats only or mostly meat.

Cartilage A flexible material found in the skeleton. It forms the entire skeleton of cartilaginous fish.

Colony A group of the same type of animals that live together.

Dislocate To move a bone out of its normal position.

Filter To sieve some particles from water or another liquid.

Gland An organ of the body that makes and releases a particular substance.

Honeycombed Made up of lots of spaces which may be filled with air.

Inflate To fill with air

Navigate To find the way.

Nocturnal Active at night.

Plankton Tiny animals and plants that float in water.

Predator A meat-eating animal that hunts and kills other creatures for food.

Pregnant When a female animal is carrying unborn young.

Prey An animal that is hunted by other animals.

Saliva The watery liquid formed in the mouth that helps to moisten food.

Savannah An area of tropical grassland.

Scavenger An animal that feeds on the remains of dead animals.

Serrated Having a jagged edge, a bit like a saw.

Solitary Living alone.

Sub-Saharan Africa A region of Africa found to the south of the Sahara desert.

Streamlined Having a smooth shape that slips easily through water.

Suffocating Stopping an animal from breathing.

Talon The long, hooked claw found on a bird of prey.

Territory A particular area that an animal lives in and defends from others.

Venomous Poisonous, producing poison or venom.